UNLOCK YOUR POWER

Unlock Your Power

DR. KIM BARBER

Black Muse Publishing

Copyright page

Unlock Your Power

ISBN: 979-8-218-36144-0 (eBook)
ISBN: 979-8-218-36143-3 (Paperback)

First Black Muse Publishing trade paperback edition May 2024
Cover art by Black Muse Publishing
All quotes associated with the chapter titles are original works of the author.

Printed by IngramSpark in the USA

www.blackmusepublishing.com

Contents

Dedication

To my worldwide, international sisterhood of phenomenal women! Allow these keys to open your door to freedom.

To my mother and father who taught me that I can do anything and I am somebody!

Foreword

At a serendipitous moment in time, Dr. Kim asked me to write the forward to Unlock Your Power. I am in the midst of my first political campaign. To be clear, this is not the first political campaign I have ever worked on or volunteered for, but it is the first campaign where I am the candidate. Dr. Kim's insight and guidance comes to me at a time when I am taking a great leap into the unknown. And, of course, as a woman, I am taking this leap with all the obligations women carry - I am running my own campaign while working full time, raising two sons, running a household, dealing with the realities of aging parents, all with the constant awareness that my husband, my children, my parents, my work need so much more from me than I have to give if I want to win this race.

The campaign is a turning point for me. I am making the choice to not cave to any of the outside interests and obligations telling me – sometimes in a whisper and sometimes very loudly – what I should or should not be doing with my time. To take the opportunity to make a difference in my community, I am using the keys Dr. Kim identifies to unlock the power inside me that is necessary to move forward. I am not listening to the voices telling me to step aside and let a man run for office.

Unlock Your Power is a gem of a book where Dr. Kim lays

out the "keys" necessary to unlock a power that lives inside you versus something that can be found on the outside. Dr. Kim combines her education, her career history, and her travels with a level of compassion and sisterhood that effectively helps women succeed. This little book is packed with personal experiences and recommendations delivered in an easy to grasp style for unleashing your power and moving forward toward a more purposeful and fulfilling life. Utilizing Dr. Kim's seven Keys to Freedom, women can live their most authentic life.

Unlock Your Power can be read for motivation and reflection as you navigate difficult periods in your life, or it can be tackled as a workbook guiding you on your personal growth journey. Either way, one guarantee is the book you are about to read has been written with one goal in mind: to provide you with the keys necessary to unlock your power so you too can live a purpose filled life.

Enjoy the ride but most of all enjoy the future you can create on this journey.

Kate Daniels
Monterey County Planning Commissioner

Introduction

The hurt of the past can drive us to a great future if we allow it to teach us.

What is your superpower? What is that special something about you that makes you unique from everyone else? If this is the first time you are thinking about the answer to these questions, you are not alone! And if you are saying to yourself, you don't have a superpower, well hold on tight, because I'm here to change your mindset.

We all have gifts and talents; just by being a woman, you have been imparted with many attributes such as being an incredible multitasker, juggling home, finances, children, pets, spouse, work, school, and the list goes on. During the COVID pandemic, you've discovered you are a homeschool teacher, tech support, and expert planner. You are imparted with discernment, a nurturing spirit, grace, and wisdom. You are resilient, able to carry your burdens and everyone else's while working tirelessly to ensure your tribe is well fed, cared for, safe, and loved. Your title and position as the CFO and **Chief Female Officer** of the Household makes you an invaluable and priceless asset.

You are all of this and more! If you've never considered your worth, I need you to see these superpowers as just the tip of the iceberg.

For many of us, we tend to handle our business so effortlessly, that it's easy to overlook just what we bring to the table. In fact, we tend to sell ourselves short because of different experiences we've had in the past or how we've been raised. If you read through this again, many of these characteristics are what is *expected* of us. And while I celebrate all of these superpowers, I have to also look at the cost!

There can be a cost for wearing that cape and suit of armor all the time, 24/7. You can easily hide behind caring and doing things for others while never focusing on yourself. I'd like to challenge you that if you actually did take time to sit still for a minute and really look inward, you may just have to admit that locked away in the depths of your soul, there is hurt, pain, abuse, disappointment, regret, neglect, sadness, and defeat. While you've become an expert at exhibiting all the aforementioned superpowers, you've also conditioned yourself to keep the real truth about your life hidden because rather than deal with it, you choose to run yourself ragged for everyone else...but yourself! And while you are excelling at the surface superpowers -- the ones expected of you -- the areas you really should be focusing on lie dormant in your soul.

That's why it's just the tip of the iceberg. There's more to you that lies beneath.

I've been birthing this book for a long time. Like two decades. This book is for all women, even the woman who has it all figured out. I applaud you and celebrate the Queens that you are. But, even when we "arrive", there are incidences of thoughts of "Am I Enough." Yes, the Imposter Syndrome. This book is also for the woman who is still searching and seeking and asking herself, "What is my purpose? Have I allowed my past to overshadow my power? Am I living for others while forsaking my own destiny?" This book is for the woman who knows they have work to do in order to live their most authentic life.

With all of my experiences of working with women from all walks of life, I know what it's like to be running past your own shadow so you don't have to face your current reality. I've worn the cape, devalued my worth, and internalized painful secrets, dying on the inside until one day, I did the work and unpacked and released all of that extra baggage I was carrying around. It was a faith walk and my connection to a higher power is what really allowed me to believe in myself and have the courage to make a change. In speaking with many other women, I found that while they seemed successful, in their secret closet, they cried tears of distress, longing for rediscovery of who they really were but weren't quite sure how to get there.

I want to help you on that journey. It's time to emerge from the shadows and learn to let go of some -- if not all of that baggage that's been packed away. Don't just settle for just surviving; praise God for that, but it's all about achieving power – your personal best.

Hope has never been as big as it is right now. As you read the following pages, my desire for you is that you find yourself and most importantly, find the right key to unlock the power that lives inside of you.

***

Key 1: Dealing with Demons in Your Suitcase

Wrestling with demons of sabotaging thoughts.

I want to share with you a true story about someone we'll call Miss Shackled. I met her when I was a teenager, still trying to find my own way in this thing called life. Miss Shackled was a very attractive young lady, but she didn't act like it, nor did she see herself in that way. We were both in dating mode, trying to find that knight in shining armor. I found myself selective and discerning (but not always right), but Miss Shackled was the opposite. The first one who gave her any type of attention would become *her man.* Sadly, I would watch her go through one after the other. She would be in and out of less than savory relationships with young men who treated her like trash. As the dutiful friend, I would be there for her, providing advice, and trying to help her see the value in herself and that she was better than these young men who could easily see her vulnerability and then proceed to take full advantage of her instability. She would agree with me, telling me I was right, but then in a few weeks, she would have a new boo and the cycle would start again.

One day I visited her home but didn't stay long. Her father was belligerent, mean, and scary. Come to find out he was drunk, an alcoholic. This was his regular state of mind. On a few more occasions when I would visit, if he was at home, I was asked to wait outside. I've never lived with an addict, but I could only imagine what that must have been like growing up in that type of situation.

I didn't know it then, but as I matured and we grew distant, I had a different perspective on her poor relationship choices. She was looking for love in all the wrong places. She was seeking a father figure, someone to protect her and take care of her like daddies are supposed to do. But because her home life was such a wreck – and who knows what else happened behind closed doors – she had nothing to fall back on as far as making good choices with men, love, and relationships.

It's important to note that her mother was indeed in the picture. Her mother did not leave the toxic environment but probably mentally succumbed to it, leaving both of them subjected to less than desirable living conditions. The origin of this could possibly have been generational, where my friend's grandmother was abused and her mother before her. What ends up happening is this type of disorder becomes normal. It becomes a habit and acceptable. For young girls, it sets in motion a false notion that all women should take abuse and just deal with it. That this is the way it is and don't you dare think differently.

Whenever Miss Shackled left that house, her load was heavy! The wheels on her rolling suitcase were bent and warped from all of the unresolved demons in her bag. In the morning, her eyes struggled to open, heavy with the weight of what the day would bring. Whether it was rain or sunshine, darkness engulfed her soul. She walked around like just a shell of herself, dragging that suitcase behind, shackled to her like an extra appendage. We're told to leave the past behind but what if the past has moved in permanently, stuck on replay? In many instances, if this goes unresolved, it can have devastating consequences such as drug abuse, resentment, isolation, depression, and even suicide.

If this is you or you know someone who is going through it, there is a light at the end of the tunnel. Let's break into the suitcase and unpack some of what has been weighing it down. I've selected just a few issues to tackle I've found to be most prevalent in my conversations with women: **Environment, Unworthy, Low Self-Esteem, and F.E.A.R.** Depending on your history, there could be multiple layers to explore, so this is just a starting point. My prayer is that once you begin to do the work, you'll find it valuable and want to continue. We'll also explore some freedom tools that can be used to not only change your immediate circumstances but will set you on the path to reshape the rest of your life.

Environment

Your environment is very conducive to your healing. As a matter of fact, **it is mandatory**. If you are in a toxic environment where you are experiencing verbal or physical abuse or you are not receiving any support, you need to immediately work on an exit plan because staying in that type of degradation will not do anything to help your circumstances or your mindset. You may be saying you don't have any money, you have nowhere to go, and no family or friends to depend on. If you have one or all of these challenges, I want to encourage you to not lean into them as impossibilities but to look at each one as a mountain that can be climbed with the right tools, faith, and courage. Changing your environment will probably be one of the hardest things you will do because like a comfy pair of shoes busting out at the seams with holes in the soles, it is still familiar, even though it is a hot mess. It is what you know...but it does not define you. Those shoes need to go! So do you. Here are five freedom tools to change your environment:

1. **Pray, Meditate, Repeat.** For me, this is #1. My faith is paramount to my existence. It directs my pathways and lights my journey. It grounds me and keeps me sane. But if you aren't a Christian, I urge you to consider meditation. Find that quiet time every day and really focus on what you want to do and where you want to be. Close your eyes and **picture your nirvana,** your ideal happy place, no matter how unachievable it may seem. Then take deep breaths. **Breathe in** hope, faith, clarity, and strength. **Exhale** pain, negativity, and defeat. Journal your thoughts and pray/reflect on them. Speak **LIFE** into your plans every day, without fail. To climb out of your hellhole, you will need to be focused because **many obstacles are going to come your way.** Praying and meditating will fortify you for the next step.

2. **Find a Support Group.** In order to make the climb, you are going to need the faith of a mustard seed and the support of committed women to help you on

your journey. There are several support groups for all walks of life. You just have to look in the right place. Here is a link to women's organizations you should check out (https://seramount.com/articles/womens-organizations-you-need-to-know/) but a Google search will also produce results. There may even be groups at your workplace or place of worship.

Also, I would add that you can make your own circle of support with your close friends and/or family. You may be saying to yourself you've never done anything by yourself, or they may look at you some kind of way and judge your presence. I challenge that defeatist mentality. If you look for excuses, they will surely appear and then you are contributing to your predicament.

3. **Sanity Savings.** A fast way to change your environment is to physically leave it, but that usually takes money. You will need to do some financial planning to be out on your own and move into a new place. Creating a savings plan will help after you map out all of the expenses you anticipate. Hiring a consultant or a financial expert is highly encouraged. One of the resources I recommend is the Concierge Financial Group. You may even have to temporarily get a second job, all the while keeping your eyes on the prize of mental and physical freedom. You should be able to contact your local small business administration for help with budgeting. If you know that starting over in a new residence is your ultimate goal, start saving towards that goal today.

4. **Escape.** Sometimes we just need a weekend to ourselves to really recharge so we can move forward. Find

a weekend getaway or longer if you can manage it. While there, relax, rejuvenate and explore what you really want or need to get out of that toxic environment. Take your journal, laptop, or tablet. If your funds are low, retreat houses are very reasonable and often include all meals. For some, having this weekend getaway from it all will allow you to declutter your mind and have a clearer picture of how to move forward.

5. **Issue Evictions**. There are occasions where we are a victim of our circumstances. We allow people into our lives who do not have our best interests at heart. We go to places we aren't really wanted, but we long to be accepted, so we keep going back hoping for a change only to get our feelings hurt. We've been unequally yoked to our partner or spouse for years and have tolerated abusive conditions for fear of being alone. Something has got to give! You need to start issuing evictions to those people, places, or things that have been detrimental to your wellbeing. I cannot make that judgment call for you, but during your quiet, meditative time, seek wisdom on how to **safely** proceed.

Unworthy

The first thing I want to tell you is that regardless of your faith association, you are beautifully and wonderfully made. You are a unique masterpiece. There is no one like you. Irrespective of what you've been told, you have a purpose and a destiny. You have been instilled with unmatched gifts and talents that are waiting to be unleashed because someone is waiting for you as your story and life's footprint will bless someone else. Do not take your dreams, hopes, and passions to the grave. It's time to declare and decree that you are more than a conqueror. You are an overcomer!

Say and post these affirmations daily until you believe them and they start to diminish and erase all of the negative seeds that have been planted within your soul. Create some of your own to add to the list.

1. When I look in the mirror, my reflection shows a beautiful flower about to bloom.
2. I am grateful to be alive and to have another day to get it right.
3. I have a purpose. I am somebody. I am more than my circumstances.
4. I am blessed and seek to be a blessing to others.
5. I have the drive and ambition to achieve my goals.
6. I deserve to be respected.
7. I am blessed and highly favored.
8. I will see life as a glass half full.
9. I am not a punching bag nor a repository for abuse.
10. Above all things, I am loved by the Creator.

Low Self-Esteem

You may think people can't see it, but there are clear signs when you are exhibiting low self-esteem. When you walk into a room, you keep your head down; when you're in a crowd, you shrink to the back; you don't make eye contact. You don't take criticism well or believe all criticism is negative; you frequently find fault with your appearance.

Low self-esteem does relate to its cousin, "Unworthy," but I want to keep this a separate topic because it requires some different tools which work together with the affirmations.

After you recite your daily affirmations, the next thing to do is to implement them. You may be asking, "What does that mean?"

Affirmations are more than just *speaking* them out loud. They require activation. I've taken a few affirmations from above and provided a way for you to make them real which, in turn, will boost your self-esteem.

1. When I look in the mirror, my reflection shows a beautiful flower about to bloom.

   - It's time for a makeover. Go to the salon or spa. Have your face professionally slayed by a make-up artist. Dress up and if you have to, go on a date with yourself. Don't make this a one-and-done! Do it as frequently as you can.

2. I am grateful to be alive and to have another day to get it right. This is about embracing your Right Now. Here are 3 options:

   - Visit the elderly. Be grateful that you have more time to live life as the Creator intended before you can no longer.
   - Re-evaluate your accomplishments and then list what you hope to do in the next 5 years and commit to being around to see them through.
   - Walk/bicycle around your neighborhood, soaking up the sunshine, raindrops, or snowflakes. Savor how blessed you are to have all your senses to enjoy the

beauty of the earth, recognizing life's simple pleasures. Be bold and do all three.

3. I have a purpose. I am somebody. I am more than my circumstances.

- There is something that you do that someone needs. Whatever that is, remind yourself daily that your services are needed and are of value, even if they are services to your family.

4. I have the drive and ambition to achieve my goals.

- Whatever your goals in life are, start planning for them. Write them down, create a vision board and then take small, incremental steps towards them being a reality.

5. I deserve to be respected.

- People will do what you allow. As soon as someone is disrespectful towards you or speaks to you in a nasty way, you should take action to either remove yourself from the situation or ask not to be spoken to in that manner. This will take courage, which will build your confidence. If a verbal approach seems intimidating, write the person a note. Discern which one is best for you but gaining self-esteem means making a conscious decision to no longer be mistreated.

6. I am not a punching bag nor a repository for abuse.

· Mental or physical abuse is never okay unless you are a professional boxer getting paid! Find a support group immediately. If you are in a volatile situation, seek the proper help as your safety is paramount. Most of all, remember that you are a diamond, a precious jewel, a royal queen, and should be treated as such.

7. Above all things, I am loved by the Creator.

· God does not make any junk and that includes you! I am a firm believer that nothing can ever separate us from God and His love for us is infinite. When you are feeling unloved and unwanted, take some intentional time to sit in a quiet, still space and meditate on your favorite scripture, song, poem, or mantra. Know that every day you have breath, you have the opportunity to transform your circumstances.

F.E.A.R

American author, Zig Ziglar, said F.E.A.R has two meanings: "Forget Everything and Run or **Face Everything and Rise.** The choice is yours!" I could not have said it better myself but let's focus on **RISING.**

Let's start by acknowledging that the feeling of fear is real. If you are afraid of heights, the thought of jumping out of a plane or riding a rollercoaster is terrifying. Some people are afraid of dogs, spiders, bees, needles, the dark, just to name a few. Fear can make you physically sick with symptoms of anxiety, heart palpitations, nervousness, sweaty hands, diarrhea, and nausea. The thing about fear is it is something that can be overcome, but like anything, it takes work. As I like to say, "Don't let your past failures or fears keep you from your future victories."

If you have fear in your suitcase, it will literally take over and demand to be in control. **Fear is a bully demon.** It says you can't change your **environment** because it will be too hard. It will keep you wrapped up in feeling **Unworthy** and contribute to your **Low Self-Esteem. Fear will start saying,** "Who do you think you are? No way you can do this. You won't make it." Your fear will keep you paralyzed and stuck, making it nearly impossible to move forward.

Some fear is innate and is there for a reason. For example, you may be around someone or something that gives you an uneasy feeling. In that case, you need that sixth sense to keep you safe.

The fear we are focusing on in this section is **the fear that is keeping you from that next level living**. It's the one(s) we want to unpack, examine and then find ways to conquer. Here are some freedom tools to assist with dealing with fear.

1. **Name it:** Whatever the fear is, call it out and acknowledge it.
2. **Listen to it:** It's going to demand attention, but what is it saying? Is it saying what you can't do? Just like it talks to you, you need to start speaking back to it that, even though you feel afraid, it will not become the center of attention or the driver of your life. Toss it to the back seat.
3. **Research it:** Investigate the fear and see what resources are available on how to conquer it. You will find you are not alone.

4. **Embrace baby steps:** Whatever your fear is, depending on how deep it is, it's going to require you to take baby steps to get through it. As you start to unpack all of the demons in your suitcase, as they come out one at a time, there will probably be another one you'll have to deal with. Realize and be okay that it's a slow jog, not a sprint. Every step forward is a step towards progress.
5. **Share it with a trusted community.** As mentioned earlier, you need to change your environment and find a group who will be there to encourage you on this journey.
6. **Celebrate the small wins.** For every victory, celebrate! Shout out loud that you've made it thus far. Journal it and feel good that you've accomplished a goal.
7. **Fail forward.** Listen...this is tough work. If it was easy, there wouldn't be so many articles, research, and topics on conquering your fears. Take your time and don't beat yourself up if you still become uneasy or afraid. As long as you are doing your best, that is all anyone can ask.

Let's do a recap: We've explored 4 demons that may be in your suitcase: **Environment, Unworthy, Low Self-Esteem,** and **F.E.A.R.** You've been given lots of freedom tools to help you change your environment, erase feelings of unworthiness, gain self-esteem, and conquer your fears. As you do the work, your bag should no longer be weighed down, as you will have unloaded and unpacked those things that had you bound. As you empty out the "rubbish," work to fill it with peace, joy, faith, love, and self-discovery.

In case you were wondering about Miss Shackled, she did eventually escape her circumstances and worked many years in therapy to reclaim her peace of mind.

Motivational Moment

This is probably going to be hard work, and I want to encourage you to love yourself through it. It's time to make yourself #1. It's really important that you engage in some self-care throughout this process. You deserve it!

Level-up Challenge

Right now at this moment, unpack one thing that has been weighing you down and start being an overcomer today. Stay engaged in the process and choose someone to keep you accountable in each step. You Can Do This!

Key 2: Unlocking Your Why

Your competency has to catch up with your calling.

No doubt you've seen or read many articles, books, or blogs on discovering your purpose. You may have even attended workshops, seminars, and conferences where finding your vocation and your goal in life was the main topic of discussion.

This is not that kind of lecture.

What I want to do is come at it from a different lens, a different angle that either builds on the lessons you've already learned or perhaps might even expand your point of view to look at your life's journey thus far in a totally different light.

It's not unusual to question who you are and why you are here, especially if you are feeling unfulfilled. I believe, though, that societal norms have tried to dictate for some of us where we should be in life, and we look at those stereotypes and end up sliding into the cookie-cutter lifestyle that has stunted the growth of many women.

Depending on how you were raised, you may have been told once you get a job, you better keep it because there is no telling when the next job will come along, or you may have been told the grass is not greener on the other side, so stay put and just endure the hardships. It gets even deeper when you have higher ambitions than your friends, family, or peers and instead of someone nurturing that spark, it's snuffed out with a fire extinguisher of negativity because why would you mess with your stability to take risks by venturing into something else?

For argument's sake, let's say you do have a great, secure job or business. You're thriving and successful, making that coin being a boss. But even with all of that, you are not completely satisfied because there are other things you want to do...there are other things gnawing away at you because at your core, you are indeed existing but not really living because you know for yourself you've only tapped into just one of the many elements you are capable of.

For some, once they reach their desired goal, it is one and done; but for many, it is not. Examples of a one-and-done could be a neurosurgeon. An attorney. An architect. A judge. A professor. But even within these disciplines, there is constant learning...and it doesn't mean those who have reached what may be considered *the pinnacle of success* do not have other aspirations waiting in the wings. The question is: Do they pursue them or forsake them? Are they really letting the world see their full potential or has the train stopped rolling because of their current success?

When I was seventeen, I immediately knew I wanted to be in the fashion industry as a fashion buyer. I just had a knack for fashion, and I was good at it! I went after it and achieved it as being one of the youngest buyers for Bloomingdales, an upscale department store. I became an Assistant Buyer and then my Lead Buyer quit unexpectedly. Even though I was put in as the interim, I was still the youngest they ever had, and I excelled in that position. After doing retail for a while, I became bored. I had already mastered all there was, and I was successful as well.

But for me, once I reached the epitome of being a buyer, other interests inside of me started to emerge.

My dad was the first African American male to become commissioner for the Maryland-National Capital Park and Planning Commission. He dealt with a lot of realtors and brokerages, so I shifted my focus to commercial real estate and enjoyed it, learning from my dad all I could. It was a good segue for me because, after Bloomingdales, I was still a young, single educated woman. However, not too much later, I became a married woman. My husband was from the Midwest, and we found ourselves relocating there. I used my brokerage skills to land an interview with a commercial real estate company. Upon my arrival at the in-person interview, the hiring managers took one look at me, and all of a sudden, they had no openings...*for a woman of color.* No, this was not explicitly stated, but it was very obvious after the positive phone response to fill the position.

I was qualified, experienced and I knew commercial real estate; I did not have my brokerage license at the time, but I had all of the other qualifications. It should be noted this position did not require a brokerage license.

I knew this field is where I was to be, so I resorted to a lot of reflection, prayer, and yes, rethinking my purpose in that season. I had landed in an environment that was not welcoming to someone of my hue or my skillset at the time, yet I still needed to make a living. I was not going backwards to retail. This is worth saying again. I was not going *backwards* to retail because that season was finished. That was in the past. It served me well, but it was not to be my future.

I hope you see some key lessons in that. Some of us can't let go of the past. We carry it around like a sack of bricks, and it can really hold you back from moving forward to the next best thing. It would have been easy for me to say, "Oh well, guess I'll go back to being a buyer." And guess what? Doing that would have given me an easy out and at the same time, a death sentence to pursuing any other purpose in fulfilling my destiny.

What was revealed to me is that sometimes your purpose may be blocked, but it does not mean it's time for you to stop going after it. It just means you need to make an adjustment as to how your gift can still serve you while navigating through uncharted waters. It does take stamina and determination, but the reward is worth it.

With the commercial real estate market seemingly issuing me a stalemate, I became a licensed residential real estate agent, and I ended up working for a renowned realtor. After a while, I continued making connections and with the help of another executive, I obtained my brokerage license.

In both cases, these were both powerhouse females who extended the hand of friendship and brought me into their world. It's worth a mention here that I'm a strong believer in the value, strength, and clout of the international sisterhood. We are to support each other as much as possible.

I became one of the first African American brokers in the community. I could have allowed the rejection to defeat me but instead, I evolved. I learned that purpose can shift depending on where you are in life and purpose can move into different areas. While to some it may have looked like

I was unfocused or unsure of what I wanted to do with my life, it was really quite the opposite. I learned to nurture my gifts, which led to my own evolution of not only personal and professional growth but keeping up with the times. Note that I mentioned *gifts*. When you have more than one gift, it is possible to have *more than one dream.*

Let's talk about your evolution. I strongly believe in order to achieve power you cannot stay the same. You must evolve so you can become relevant. In other words, you may have to reinvent yourself. I could use mega-companies such as Apple, Google, or Amazon as examples, as these companies have demonstrated evolution and staying power over the years, but I'm going to throw some love in another direction: Popeyes Chicken.

Yes, I'm talking about chicken. Who knew that "perfecting" a fried chicken sandwich would cause such an uproar for those who love chicken? When it debuted, Popeye's restaurants were sold out of chicken sandwiches for days. People were standing in lines wrapped around the corner for a chicken sandwich. Fights broke out over a chicken sandwich! What in the world? What was even more amazing is that Popeye's was already known for having good fried chicken...but someone in a test kitchen said, "It's time to step our game up."

They did not stay the same. They evolved.

I need to digress just a bit more and talk about Mr. Denzel Washington, a very fine, famous, award-winning African American actor. Do you also remember who received the Academy Award for Best Actor in 2002? That award went to Denzel for the movie Training Day.

Training Day was so much against his character type. I believe Denzel took that role because he needed to show that he was not a one-trick pony; he could play a bad guy as well as a good guy, and he could make you believe it. He did not want to be remembered only for the sweet, handsome, charismatic star that he still is today. He wanted to show depth and range so he could be looked at not just for one type of role but for many types of characters.

He created his own pathway. He also evolved.

Sometimes a person who dabbles in multiple ventures is deemed unfocused and indecisive, which is another roadblock for those who struggle with pursuing their other gifts.

I have some **Breaking News** for you. Your WHY has levels.

Without levels, there is no growth.

Without growth, there is stagnation.

And with stagnation comes complacency.

When this occurs, it's easy to bypass the work needed to discover your why because you've been duped into thinking where you are right now is where you are supposed to be indefinitely. Couple that with lack of support, and you start to believe that your only purpose in life is what you are doing right now and that just ain't so!

Let me say there is nothing wrong if you are happy and content. That is also very important to know that you are in a good place. I'm just letting you know you can have more than one WHY in this life, and it's okay to embrace it. Stop questioning what you know to be true and if you have different roads to travel, do not delay getting to your next destination. You can be grateful for where you are right now but still have the ambition to do more because of the gifts inside.

With my own journey, after I got my licenses, I opened my own brokerage company with a partner, who I'll call Susan. We focused on helping first-time home buyers, assisting with credit, first-time loans, new homeowner classes, and so on. Then later I opened my own brokerage and development company where my husband handled the development side.

During this time, I felt another shift coming on. I remember the education system where I lived lacked equity, diversity, and inclusion, and I had two African American sons in the school system. On more than one occasion, I had to go report at the school and advocate for my sons. But something in my spirit asked me, "What about the other students?" Quite frankly, I felt my plate was full, but it did not stop many ideas from rising to the top about how I could help other kids in similar situations.

After some intense soul searching, I ended up starting my own educational nonprofit, and it was to serve high school students in underserved populations. This purpose evolved out of a need, and it tapped into my passion for education. I could help my son and others too. Setting up this nonprofit was super challenging. I had to do a lot of networking and get the local government and school officials on my side. And you better believe there were people waiting for me to fail, but when you are walking in your purpose, that is what will keep you going.

One thing led to another and in a dream, I was prompted to go for my Ph.D. I obtained my Ph.D. in Public Policy and Social Change a few years later.

While my businesses were thriving in the Midwest, I attended a women's leadership meeting and met a close friend who was from California. I really liked the West Coast style of living, but I could not see us actually living there anytime soon. In the meantime, I knew my next objective was to work at a college or university. I truly enjoyed working with youth and young adults. After applying to many universities, I became a finalist at Purdue University near my residence, which I thought was my nirvana of schools. This was after a lot of "no's." I had applied to many opportunities with no success, and if you think about it too hard, it will discourage you.

You have to build a thick skin when moving in a purposeful direction. Be ready to face opposition and find your own enthusiasm. I got to a point where I stopped dwelling on NO and turned that into **NOT YET**, so I flipped the script. I started welcoming the NO. I knew my yes was coming.

While waiting for my YES from Purdue, California State University called me out of the blue and they wanted me down there quickly. At first, I was hesitant but then it became sparkling clear that's where I was supposed to go, and doors started opening for me immediately. I have not looked back since, and it has been one of the best decisions for me and my family.

I've also formed my own community for young women and college students: **Journey To Becoming**. I started this community to transform lives by supporting and leading women and university students to fulfill their purpose. Additionally, I added and zoned into the mantle that is upon me by creating my brand (Dr. Kim), yes, you guessed it's called, "Unlock Your Power." It is a woman empowerment experience. To empower women (all over the world) in challenging circumstances by unlocking their inner strength through self-discovery, turning their adversity into strength.

This is where I am currently in life, but it does not mean this is my finale.

Now when you ponder about your why and existence in the universe, I hope this has shown you that your why does not have to be one-dimensional. Also, if you've paid attention to my trajectory thus far, I mastered each one of my gifts before really leaping to the next. So it's not about being a worn-out multitasker. Your why is something that is not contentious or gives you grief. Instead, it's about digging into what feeds your soul at the moment and excelling at it past your wildest dreams so that when you do move to the next moment, you will have left a solid legacy behind – a firm foundation that can be built upon for your greater good.

Motivational Moment

Embrace all of your various gifts and talents. No matter where you are in life, you are needed in the capacity you are in. There will be challenges and haters along the way, so be encouraged to stay the course knowing your life has purpose and what you bring to the table will be unlike anyone else.

Level UP Challenge

Write down all of your interests, even things you have often thought about but never acted on. Select one interest and research it as if you were to make it come to fruition. This will activate your purpose and the mind shift needed to propel you to your next WHY.

Key 3: The Journey to Self-Discovery

Know your purpose; don't just exist.

Hopefully, you're still on the journey with us. Remember the discovery is in the journey, not the destination. Let me just remind you that regardless of what anyone has told you, you are brilliant. There's no one like you. Even identical twins have unique characteristics that set them apart from one another. They complement each other, just like your gifts and talents balance with others' gifts and talents to reach desired goals and dreams.

I firmly believe we are not designed to go through life alone or in a bubble. There is strength in numbers. There is power in the sisterhood, each one of us intricately linked through our capabilities and expertise to finding that common ground. And once we find that commonality, we use it to nurture those relationships so that no sister is left behind!

Before we move on, let's take a few moments. An intentional pause. Find a quiet place to center yourself and allow your mind to be free. Take deep breaths in and out a few times. Then close your eyes for a few seconds. Mentally visualize your "**Right Now.**" Now visualize your "**New Horizon.**" Your New Horizon could be a new job, new house, international travel, public speaking, higher education, entrepreneurship, and so on. You may have more than one aspiration and if so, that is excellent because it shows you have something you are still striving towards.

Don't worry about the financial means, the time allotment, or the "how" of it all. The point is to allow yourself to dream and dream big! As long as you have the ability to dream, **you have purpose**! The pathway will be manifested based on your will to succeed.

I'm a firm believer that with consistent and intentional prayer, meditation, and/or reflection – whatever your preference -- focusing on where you are now and where you want to be is a necessary part of the journey, along with **knowing who you are** and how you fit into the bigger life picture. When we can't see ourselves on life's stage, we start to feel like we don't belong, or we struggle to see our rightful place. Trust and believe you are relevant, and to get even more clarity, we're about to jump into self-discovery. This is a deeper dive into your "why." It's peeling back the layers of your outer shell and examining the core of your existence.

Consider this your inner vision examination. Within the next few pages, we're going to review a few of the unlimited possibilities of your true purpose. These gems are actually roles or positions you have mastered, whether intentionally through schooling or innately. It's important that you self-identify with one or more of them so you can be better positioned in life, at your company, in your home, or in the marketplace. But also so you can know who you are! As you read them, note which of these gems speaks to you the most. I'm sure you will find yourself in one of these...and if not, create your own.

Bridge Builder

If you are a Bridge Builder, you can scan a room and see all of the puzzle pieces and how they fit together. You connect people who would complement each other, seeing a win-win for both sides. The Bridge Builder can link people to get to their purpose or their goals. You are behind the scenes, weaving connections that have amazing value, but it's rare that you are thanked. Bridge Builders do not expect anything in return.

Where We Might See You

You tend to be at networking events, trade shows, large conferences, high-profile events, or other venues that allow you to interact with people.

Bridge Builder's Characteristics

You are a people person and very resourceful. You have a dynamic personality and take initiative. Talking to strangers, as well as familiar people comes easy to you. You have a lot of contacts. Your knowledge is deep. Basically, you KNOW people.

Why Bridge Builders Are Needed:

It is said there are 7 degrees of separation. A Bridge Builder will make it only one!

Supporter

As a Supporter, you are the person who shows up day or night and lends a helping hand. You don't complain and you are an *uber volunteer*. Supporters get energy from what they do. You are the first to arrive and often the last to leave, filling in any gaps. You are the one in the front row, cheering on your bestie, peer, family member, or business associate.

Where We Might See You

You are there all the time at every event possible, at the door, being an usher, taking tickets, decorating tables, serving food, doing last-minute trips to the store, taking pictures, working out issues, and whatever else is needed to help out. Additionally, you are also found right beside your friends. You are the one that is there whenever they are in need.

Your Characteristics

You are a natural helper and are very dependable. You aren't there for fame or glory. You're there because you get joy from watching people succeed. You are the first person to buy whatever they are selling. You lend your time, talent, and energy. You are the *ride or die*. When schedules don't permit for everyone else, you are there.

Why You are Needed:

The Supporter is needed because your heart is truly filled with joy at being in service. You do it selflessly and without monetary payment. Just being there is pay-ment enough. You are needed because without you, certain things wouldn't happen. You quietly build confidence and hold everything together behind the scenes. Having you there makes a big difference, as there is nothing like looking out and seeing your Supporter there, in your corner. You are significant!

Creative

Innovation is the Creative's mantra. You find ways to do things that no one else dares think about. The Creative person has visionary qualities. Others can't see the whole picture, but you see it from a different dynamic. Creatives like to plan and invent. You like to put pieces together and think outside of the box vs. a cookie-cutter approach. You offer a different way to see colors, bringing sunshine to an otherwise dull landscape.

Where We Might See You

You are in museums, theaters, art shows, bakeries, events, parties, fashion, publishing, architecture, education, business, and much more. In the workplace, you are the lead for tasks such as organizing big events and running programs with innovative ideas. Also, you may be found in artistic positions such as creating promotional materials, designing fashion, birthing new ideas, in political campaigns, creating websites, and engaging social media posts.

Your Characteristics

You thrive on change, but also like having space to think, create and just be you. Your work hours are probably flexible, feeding into your creative sphere. On occasion, you may be seen as eclectic, aloof, or flamboyant...and you have no misgivings about it. You like to be appreciated and thrive on change. You are out of the box and can present different ideas in different settings – from abstract to targeted.

Why You are Needed

You bring a new perspective and a breath of fresh air to whatever you are involved in. You allow us to see things through your eyes. If you really think about it, without the Creative in place, movies, theater, television, or the Steve Jobs of this world would not exist! Steve Jobs stated, "Innovation distinguishes between a leader and a follower." Creatives are the catalyst for dreams.

Planner

If planning is your vocation, you are all about organization. You keep projects on course. Everything is well thought-out and in order. Planners can easily see where there are gaps or holes in a particular process. Planners, like the creative, have some visionary attributes as well. Your organizational skills are top-notch, and you can easily map out all the details necessary for success. You are called upon to keep things on track but allow people to see what's possible and all the labor and moving parts needed to make it work out. You see the fine print and bring it to life.

Where We Might See You

You are at the forefront of any project or event. So many things fall through the cracks without a plan, so your role is pivotal. Having a plan design is crucial to the event, business, or project's success.

Your Characteristics

You are extremely organized, detailed oriented, and meticulous. Some might say you are anal or have obsessive-compulsive disorder (OCD) characteristics, but these work to your advantage. You are flexible and able to nuance plans to accommodate the project's needs. There are several types of planners. The two you may be familiar with are the Goal-oriented Planner and the Detailed-oriented Planner. The goal-oriented planner sees the vision and the end game. They push people to get to the finish line. They make sure people are lined up to assist with getting to the goal and that everyone is clicking on all cylinders. The detail-oriented planners are really into the details; their focus is on all of the bullet points that fall under each task that is assigned to a particular process or project. Their energy and focus are in the details, though the outcome is the same.

Why You are Needed

We need Planners. Without you, there is chaos. That blueprint is crucial to our success and without it, we're left to our own devices. The plan keeps us accountable and on track. You are the backbone to success.

Encourager

You are the one who is *thee* biggest cheerleader. Encouragers lift others up with affirmations and compliments. You give off positive vibes. You are that espresso shot, that energizer, and the one who pushes us on, even when we've given up.

Where We Might See You

Oftentimes, you show up when we're at our lowest point. Your intuition and general connectedness to who we are allows you to be available just when we need you most. We may not see you every day, but once you do show up and drop those golden nuggets of wisdom, it gives us the strength to carry on. You bring energy to a project, business, or person.

Your Characteristics

You are usually in those places and spaces, behind the scenes, until called into service. You have a kind heart, instinctive spirit, and know just the right things to say to help someone overcome any obstacles.

Why You are Needed

You are needed because we all need a quick pick-me-up. You provide that extra *oomph* to get us over the hump. There is not a lot of encouragement going around these days, so we need you in our lives more than ever. We need your spark in projects, schools, businesses, and in our world!

Leader

Leaders are sprinkled with a lot of characteristics of the visionary. You see the destination and the goal. You are the one who rallies the troops, provides them with all the tools they need but also will jump in to help without hesitation. You know you are only as good as the team, and you have no problem letting the team shine.

Where We Might See You

You are everywhere! Every project has a leader aka manager, supervisor, team lead, or director. In the home, mothers and fathers are leaders. In your places of worship, businesses, universities, on your committees or groups, even in the homeowner's association, there is a leader.

Your Characteristics

Leaders have a desire to succeed and also know they are setting an example for the rest to follow. You care deeply about your team. Leaders are trustworthy and agile. You also know how to foster teamwork and productivity by being good listeners and providing pathways to success.

Why You are Needed

Without someone like you skilled in driving the train, it will derail, crash and burn. Enough said!

Visionary

Visionaries are the big picture people. You can see where no one else can see. A visionary sees past the roadblocks. You dream big and continue to refresh your imagination with new ideas and fresh thinking. You are somewhat of a risk-taker and believe strongly in what you perceive. You may fail and if that happens, you can immediately reset it and start again. It may not be perfect, but you can express what you need to get to your destination. Others may see a wall while you, the visionary, see what's **INSIDE** the wall.

Where We Might See You

You are at Apple, Google, IBM, higher education institutions, think tanks, and boardrooms. You have ideas for entrepreneurship in your psyche. You created a vision of at-home food delivery boxes. You said we could fly to the moon or drive electric cars. You design emergency pop-up housing or create new currencies. You are in meetings with your vision board and plans, seeing well into either an immediate or distant future. You are creating new medications and vaccines. You are the pie in the sky, and we always want a slice!

Your Characteristics

Fearless, revolutionary, calm, idealist...these are just some of your attributes. Sometimes you align closely with the Creative. You are strategic to a point, but you are not frugal. There is something magical about watching you work because your ideas are limitless.

Why You are Needed

You are vital! Having vision gives us hope. When things look bleak, a Visionary will show us the possibilities. Without a vision, there is no tomorrow, next week, or next year. You, as a Visionary, are ahead of the game. While people are waiting for the next big thing, you have already figured out how to create it. Visionaries shoot for the moon and if they land amongst the stars, at least they aimed high.

***

I hope you see yourself in one or more of these roles. In your tribe, you really should be surrounding yourself with these types of jewels. At least one of these personality types should be in your circle of trust. Surrounding yourself with like-minded people, meaning people who think just like you, will not allow you to grow, so seek to expand your circle not focusing on the size of your tribe but the **quality** of its members. This does not mean that you have core values and goals that are similar. (Not necessarily the same goals).

So...which one or more of these gems are you? Whatever it is, give it life and let it shine!

Motivational Moment

How do we get to the next level of our purpose without knowing who we really are? We are all striving and improving ourselves. That's where evolving comes in. With me, it's with God's help. For you, it might be through something else. Whatever it is, activate it today.

Level UP Challenge

For all of my BOSS ladies, I dare you to do this challenge: Ask someone else -- a friend or family member – which one of these gems do they believe you to be. Then diversify and ask three different people. Don't forget, as we've learned you can have different avatars, so don't get fixated on just one.

Food for thought: Did the answers surprise you or provide confirmation? Note the outcome. Your top three will illuminate your inner vision identity.

Key 4: The Key to Overcoming Haters

Peace is something you have to intently create in your world daily.

Now, this chapter right here...take heed and take notes! We are about to expose the Haters!

What is a hater?

· A person who thrives on criticizing others
· Those who have intense hostility or create divisiveness
· People full of envy

These are just some of the definitions that describe being a hater. Haters are **real**. They exist, both male and female alike. They thrive on planting negativity and discord, especially when it appears to them that others are moving forward while leaving them behind. If they are not the center of attention, then no one else can be either. They do not celebrate when it relates to others' success.

When I was in middle school, I thought everyone was in my corner. There was a person I thought was my friend. We used to hang out. Next thing I know, I was accused of stealing her boyfriend and she turned on me quickly. Never even asked for my side of the story. Now listen, nothing can be stolen that doesn't want to be stolen, but that wasn't even the case. I didn't even know her boyfriend. Some other girls created this lie so I could be jumped after school due to their jealousy of me. And, by the way, I wasn't that type of person. I went to school, minded my business, and excelled in my studies. I was always confident with my lessons and carried myself with class due to my upbringing. But that was perceived by others as being "conceited." So from an early age, I knew what being around haters felt like and it didn't stop there.

As an adult, I had a friend copy my every move. For example, when I had a baby, she had a baby. When I bought a house, so did she. I had a second child, she got pregnant too. If I cut my hair into a bob, guess what? So did she!

This is a different form of hating. It was not for flattery. It was to show that what I was doing wasn't so special and to prove that they were going to stay on my heels and *keep me in my place.*

The hater finds it extremely difficult to just be happy for another person's success. They look for flaws and enjoy pointing them out to you but not in a respectful kind of way. They tend to embarrass you both privately and in public and will act naïve and innocent about their actions.

On the job, my peers have not wanted to see me get promoted, and I'm talking about people who I considered my friends, who I went to lunch and dinner with. Those same people saw me move up quickly and their attitude changed. Suddenly they became distant and wouldn't even give me the time of day. When I advanced in my career, they couldn't even offer up so much as a "congratulations." In other words, they were hating on my success.

I'm sharing these experiences with you so that you know that no matter where you are in life – regardless of your wealth status, prestige or influence, there are going to be those who don't have your back or who will not support your efforts. Some haters will be wolves in sheep's clothing, staying close to you just to see what you are doing. Some of these people will be those who are true supporters and want to be under your wing to learn and grow. But unfortunately, there may be those who are there just to see what goes wrong, and even try to thwart your plans. They simply do not have your best interest at heart because something in their spirit prevents them from enjoying the journey with you.

Sadly, there are a lot of broken people in our world. Unless we grew up with them or have intimate knowledge, we do not know how they've been hurt, about their afflictions, or what transpired in their historical make-up that has caused them to begrudge another's achievements.

We can't change them or their personality, but what we can definitely do is protect our personal space. But before we do that, we have to first try to identify who the haters are in our midst. Here are some tips to assist with that process:

- Discernment. Take some time to discern and identify who you can trust. You can't tell everything to everybody.

- **Positivity.** Surround yourself with positivity in your immediate circle. Note that your circle doesn't have to be a lot of people, but you need the *right* people.
- **Stay Vigilant.** Be wise in your approach, especially with new friends. Don't divulge all of your plans before doing your own internal vetting process.
- **Naysayers.** In group settings, be mindful of nonverbals, those who rarely have anything positive to say about your suggestions or ideas.
- **Silent Observer.** Be a quiet observer and take inventory of those who tend to see the glass half full where you are concerned and rarely offer anything constructive. For me, I had to watch and pray. That helped me with my haters. You can learn a lot by being quiet.

Other places where haters tend to reside are on social media. Social media can be a blessing and a curse. There are people who are cyber-stalkers, just watching and waiting for you to stumble and fail. They may even sign up for your events, live streams, and podcasts, but are there to just be critical.

Just like how you detox your body, you need to detox your life and your "friends" list. Take inventory and do a thorough cleansing and purge the poison out. Oftentimes we know *just who the culprits are*, but we let our feelings get in the way.

For those people you think fall into this category, start asking yourself these reflection questions:

- Do they come with good vibes?
- Are they supportive and a cheerleader?
- Do they add value to your life?

· Do they seem to rejoice when you fail or struggle?

For some, this process will be tough but very necessary. Take time to meditate and reflect on what is important. Let the "Block", "Delete", and "Unfollow" become standard actions in your daily life, and once you identify those people, there's no need to be nasty or violent. Just ease them on down the road. It's all about protecting your mental and physical space. Some people you have to love from a distance.

Now be sure not to confuse haters with tough love and hard truths from your sister-friends who speak assertively. This constructive criticism is always expressed with love, care, and mutual respect. We all need some truth-tellers in our lives.

It's time to start issuing some evictions and letting go of those who mean you harm and then replace that vacancy with the right kind of people who will sow good vibes into your mind, body, and soul.

Motivational Moment

Don't let haters be your excuse for not succeeding. That is not your excuse anymore because you have the power to protect your peace at all costs. Haters may make you cry, but don't let them see you sweat! Slay the haters with your sword of victory.

Level UP Challenge

Time to conduct a human detox and start issuing some digital evictions. Who in your crew needs to be moved to the outer circle and beyond? The ones who are ready to go there, do it. If not, come back to it when you're ready.

Key 5: Perfection Rejection

We are not striving for perfection, we're striving for improvement.

"Sing it again!" the vocal coach demanded of the choral group that had already sung the song eight times in a row in preparation for an evening performance several days away. The melodious rhythms blended as each choral section of sopranos, altos and tenors lifted their voices like never before to new heights surpassing the heavens; yet they were singing with such fear of missing one note, taking the wrong breath, saying "ooo" instead of "ahhh", the internal joy of the performers became nonexistent with the constant desire to please the director. The piano player pounded the keys, blinded by her sweaty brow, afraid to lift a finger to turn the page for the next sequence, relying on memory for the next stanzas. Exhaustion consumed the assembly with throats raw and raspy, yet they hit every note with exquisite precision and when the last note was sung, the deafening silence was followed by the director's stunning four words: "You can do better."

The choral group had clearly gone above and beyond to do everything in their power to please the director, but their amazing efforts still fell short.

Some could argue that such a performance *should be* top-notch and error-free, but at what point does the perfectionist mentality cause more harm than good?

Let's understand there are varying degrees to being a perfectionist. You may have this trait, thinking it's one of your strengths; instead, it can be a self-sabotaging type of gift. It's almost a disguise and that's what makes it dangerous. Until you recognize it, it will remain unchecked and not only work against you but also those you interact with as well.

I was the last one to find out I was a perfectionist. I can picture some of you cringing at the thought of me mirroring the characteristics of the choral director, however, my perfectionist attitude was primarily focused inward. Dealing with a leader who is a perfectionist will be addressed later on in this chapter.

The way I found out I had this trait was through one of my professors. While pursuing my Ph.D., I had to have an A in every class. I would be upset if it looked any different. There was a time when I received a 3.99 and I was not happy. That one percent affected me like the sky was falling, and I fought hard to get it changed, to no avail, and it bothered me for weeks. It created a lot of self-doubt and questioning of my abilities, missing out on that tiny one percent.

When he enlightened me about my being a perfectionist, I actually did not receive it because I didn't even recognize it, so I tested out his assessment with my friends.

To my great surprise, they agreed.

Being a perfectionist can have a negative connotation, so upon hearing that confirmation, my guard immediately went up. Saying you're a perfectionist tends to translate into:

1. You are inflexible
2. Your way is the best way
3. There is no way to please you
4. No one can do it as well as you can
5. You can't tolerate others' mistakes

I can say for me, these behaviors were not true. In all that I do, I am striving to be the best ME I can be. Being a perfectionist doesn't have to be detrimental to others, but it can be detrimental to you. Part of my upbringing shaped and molded me to always aim for the stars with high marks. My father and mother were very instrumental in shaping my mindset to achieve power in all that I did, and I believe part of that stemmed from us being people of color.

As women and women of color for many years, and even today, we have to *come correct*, especially in business circles where the "good old boys' club" can still reign supreme and women are not seen as true players of the game (or women are not taken seriously.) They are looking for us to stumble, be unprepared, lack knowledge, and professionalism. Even with being successful entrepreneurs, we have to prove that we're worthy of small business loans, putting together business plans, sales and marketing, contract negotiations, and presentations. At the academic level, women receiving tenure are still not at the level of male professors, even though women's skill set and/or academic achievements far outweigh their male counterparts.

As you may recall earlier in the book, I mentioned that I was involved with real estate. I had to come up with my A-game because it was a male-dominated field at that time. Someone else may bring mediocracy and be received, but as a woman of color, I had to be triple ready.

But even when you come up with that mentality, you may not be accepted. Over time, I built up a solid foundation within myself where my faith and affirmations helped to sustain me.

Dealing with so many barriers can force us to develop a perfectionist mentality because we HAVE to outshine, out-compete and outmaneuver everyone just to be recognized and if we don't, we risk being or feeling like a failure. I learned later on that in trying to achieve perfection, you would always be chasing unicorns, but focusing on **excellence** is a much healthier approach because it's showcasing the best of who you are.

We all have character flaws because no one is perfect, regardless of what you may see in the media. Unfortunately, the media has done us a grave disservice by misrepresenting reality.

Media or advertisements tend to mostly portray only model types. Women or young girls who are exposed to this consistently can suffer from low self-esteem and see themselves as "less than" if they don't meet the size requirements of being a size two or size four or have flawless skin or perfect teeth. Not everyone is supposed to be a size two, but the media will have you not loving the skin you're in and finding faults where there is none.

Some retailers and brands are coming around, though, with trying to change the narrative. Kudos to the Fenty brand by music superstar Rhianna, who has truly hit the nail on the head with a strong, diverse representation of multicultural models of all shapes and sizes. **This is Us.**

Social media is another culprit of only showing a "picture perfect" lifestyle and at one point or another, we are ALL guilty of it. We won't even put ourselves on our social media when we're down, sick, going through tribulations, have unruly hair, or sans makeup. We only post when everything is sunshine and blue skies. It's whatever we want to portray to the public. Even this is a form of perfectionism because we don't want to show there is another, less than perfect side.

Perfection cannot exist because no one is perfect.

Perfectionism also can prevent you from achieving your goals. It can become a stumbling block, instilling self-doubt where you start to berate yourself with feelings of being worthless or inadequate.

Some years back, I was producing an event and I was obsessing over it, that it was just not going to be good. It consumed every waking thought; I had issues trusting others to do it my way, and I found myself running ragged until it affected my mental and physical health through:

1. Lost sleep
2. High anxiety
3. Short-tempered
4. Double-triple check everything

I had to learn to navigate these waters and deal with it head-on and by dealing with it, I really mean *dealing with myself.* If things didn't go as planned, I've learned to ask myself this one question: Did I give my best and did I go above and beyond? If the answer is yes, then I had to learn *to let go.* Of course, I would glean the lessons learned and note areas for improvement but dwelling on the mistakes that probably went unnoticed by the average person is not beneficial.

You have to forgive yourself if something didn't go exactly right. Once you address it, identify the cause of your discomfort; then affirm it and move forward so you can get back on track with the journey.

Affirmations come in handy when we are struggling. It's good to affirm yourself, as was mentioned previously because sometimes we have to encourage ourselves and recognize that our best IS good enough.

Remember our choral director at the beginning of this chapter? Some of the people we work with who are in leadership roles exhibit this leadership style of pushing people to the edge of the cliff and telling them to "jump." After a while, it can be draining and discouraging. No matter how much browbeating is done, they will not get any more results out of them because the well has run dry.

Sometimes these types of leaders have their own inner demons they are working out and part of it is proving they belong, they can lead, and they want to be the best. The problem is they have not yet realized or admitted they are a perfectionist and can't see how their methods are alienating those who they need the most.

Here are some tips for working with a perfectionist, but keep in mind that until the person knows or admits this as their "burden," it might be super challenging.

1. Find out what their expectations are of you. If you don't agree, meet so you can both come to an agreement.

2. If you've done everything agreed upon and it is still not meeting their satisfaction, note what aspects of the final product did not meet expectations and then review those again with the leader.
3. Try to stay optimistic, pointing out everything that went well and, if available, bring the opinions of others who had positive things to say.
4. To keep your momentum going, check with other leaders/peers. In most cases, you will find you did an outstanding job, and the other person is the *known* problem.

If you do everything well, and I mean exceptionally well, they just may not receive it. That is the toxicity of being a perfectionist. You would probably have to do some soul-searching on whether or not to continue in the same position.

At this point, you may have just discovered you are a perfectionist on one or multiple levels. You can now join the club with me of being a Recovering Perfectionist. It's time to let some things go. Instead of a 12-step recovery program, here are 7 steps to manage your perfectionism.

1. First be able to understand you can strive and survive without aiming for perfection.
2. Identify what is self-sabotaging when things go awry, such as redoing everything to a fault, sleepless nights, second-guessing, and so on. These are toxic weeds that will choke out anything good.
3. Ask, meditate, and reflect on:
   a. What are you trying to achieve and is it with excellence?

    b. Do you have the bandwidth?

    c. Remember what you have control over and what you don't. Excellence still leads to success.

4. Be affirming to yourself and remember you are your worst critic. Give yourself time to develop a new way of thinking.

5. Find coping mechanisms for dealing with your perceived failures. These could be things like dinner with friends, a spa day, one-day retreats, eating your favorite food – things that bring you joy to help you move forward.

6. Journal your thoughts and try to note all of the positive things that transpired.

7. If you are a leader, admit and engage with your circle to assist with managing your expectations. They can call you out and help you with your recovery.

Remember to reject perfection and embrace excellence.

Motivational Challenge

It's worth repeating there's nothing wrong with striving for excellence. If you did your absolute best, pat yourself on the back and keep it moving.

Level Up

Are you a perfectionist? You better ask somebody. This is not a reality show. It's time to uncover the real deal and release those toxic chains.

Key 6: Harnessing Your Power

Knowledge is potential Power, but knowledge with action is Real Power!

There is nothing more exciting to watch than when a woman knows her power. We as women have that unique ability to turn heads when we walk into a room, to lead successful teams to victory, to make a way out of no way, all while holding down the fort at home, sometimes alone. As women, our instincts are unmatched. We have a natural ability to multitask, negotiate and change hearts and minds. If a woman has confidence, you can see it. There is something that moves people when you walk with confidence. When you are confident, you have nothing to prove. You don't need validation. Your non-verbals speak louder than your expressions.

We can express all these things and more...if we understand our power and what it can do!

Up until now, I've provided several keys to help build your self-esteem, discover your gifts, unpack demons, deal with haters and manage perfection. Now you have to learn how to move them into ACTION.

You may be thinking you are not ready, but you have everything it takes to win and win big! You have to shift your position from the back of the line to the leader of the pack! The *back of the line* in this case means putting yourself last and everything else first. It means holding on to those doubts and fears and letting that keep you in the shadows. It is allowing and supporting everyone else's dreams, hopes and desires while yours slips away in the wind.

In other words, you GIVE AWAY your power instead of using it for yourself! Really let that sink into the depths of your soul.

Power for some is egotistical, controlling, or narcissism. These are a few negative connotations that can be associated with power. But what I desire for you to see is that power **gives energy** to an otherwise dull meeting; it is a **life-giving source** to an unproductive team. It is the **spark** to new and innovative ideas. Power is also the energy that will pull you out of a black hole of depression or disappointment. When all seems dim, power becomes **the generator**, lighting the way so you can lead others to power.

Using all of the keys provided, it's time to activate and claim your power. You must believe it to receive it. No, this is not just a cliché, it is an action. Nothing and no one can do this for you. It already resides inside of you and will remain dormant if you allow it.

We've discussed the importance of affirmations. Affirm yourself daily by breathing life into what you want to see manifested. Remind yourself of your power and plug into all that has been learned along the way. The culmination of your experience, expertise, and knowledge is not to be taken for granted. Sometimes you need to revisit your CV/ resume to see all that you have accomplished. I encourage you to update your resume every six months; if nothing changes year after year, that is a sign you may want to consider taking classes or learning a new skill, which only adds to what you have to offer.

We previously spoke about finding the right circle of family, friends, or supporters. My family and friends would always remind me of what I have achieved, which gives that extra boost that we all need. Our human nature tends to focus on the past or what we've done wrong. Looking in that rearview mirror will always show you what you've already done; however, along with any mistakes that may have occurred, there were also victories. Examining the past will show you how you were able to persevere and make it through and for most of us, that was no easy feat. Seeing how you weathered some of life's storms to where you are now shows resilience and that should fuel your power.

How serious are you about making a difference in your personal and professional development? Actions speak louder than words. Yes, this is a popular phrase, but it's also true. I want you to grow into the gorgeous bouquet of power you were meant to be vs. being stuck on the side of a mountain.

What action(s) have you taken? If you make a decision to do nothing, that is an **action**, and it won't get you up and over that mountain. Mountains can represent a multitude of things like job promotion, entrepreneurship, academic pursuit, self-confidence, self-esteem, and so on. There is no magic potion or overnight fix. It requires work and a strategic and intentional desire for change.

Inaction leads to no growth and complacency. Reserving your power until the *right time* is not just doing yourself a disservice, but you are blocking someone else's blessing! Your gifts are not just for you. We are all here to help each other and someone is waiting for you to show up. You have to bring your best self no matter where you go. You have to command your space. You are an integral link in the circle of life and when you exude your power, others will see it and they will be encouraged and inspired. Once you know more about yourself, you will touch everyone else's life in a positive way.

The other aspect of this self-development work is flexing your **mental muscle**. Working on your inner self requires consistent and deliberate actions where you are constantly pouring in good vibes to stay fortified and encouraged. You also need to take some time to power down so you can power up! We all need time to recharge and in those moments of recharging and reflection, allow yourself permission to pamper your mind, body, and soul so you can return rejuvenated and energized.

Within this book, you've been provided **Motivational Moments** and **Level-up Challenges**. Each one was designed to help you reflect, act, and elevate. Combined, they are stepping-stones to help you navigate the obstacles of life. Just like anything else, the more you work at it, the more you will improve. If you have not completed all of the actions, try to make that a priority because the more you unpack, the more you will uncover. For your convenience, they are here below. Highlight what you need to complete and put a checkmark next to completed tasks.

Reflection

KEY 1

Motivational Moment: This is probably going to be hard work, and I want to encourage you to love yourself through it. It's time to make yourself #1. It's really important that you engage in some self-care throughout this process. You deserve it!

Level-up Challenge: Right now in this moment, unpack one thing that has been weighing you down and start being an overcomer today. Stay engaged in the process and choose someone to keep you accountable in each step. You Can Do This!

KEY 2

Motivational Moment: Embrace all of your various gifts and talents. No matter where you are in life, you are needed in what capacity you are in. There will be challenges and haters along the way, so be encouraged to stay the course knowing your life has a purpose and what you bring to the table will be unlike anyone else.

Level-up Challenge: Write down all of your interests, even things you have often thought about but never acted on.

Select one interest and research it as if you were to make it come to fruition. This will activate your purpose and the mind shift needed to propel you to your next WHY.

KEY 3

Motivational Moment: How do we get to the next level of our purpose without knowing who we really are? We are all striving and improving ourselves. That's where evolving comes in. With me, it's with God's help. For you, it might be through something else. Whatever it is, activate it today.

Level-up Challenge: For all of my BOSS ladies, I dare you to do this challenge: Ask someone else -- a friend or family member – which one of these gems do they believe you to be. Then diversify and ask three different people. Don't forget, as we've learned you can have different avatars, so don't get fixated on just one.

KEY 4

Motivational Moment: Don't let haters be your excuse for not succeeding. That is not your excuse anymore because you have the power to protect your peace at all costs. Haters may make you cry, but don't let them see you sweat! Slay the haters with your sword of victory.

Level-up Challenge: Time to conduct a human detox and start issuing some digital evictions. Who in your crew needs to be moved to the outer circle and beyond? The ones who are ready to go there, do it. If not, come back to it when you're ready.

KEY 5

Motivational Moment: It's worth repeating there's nothing wrong with striving for excellence. If you did your absolute best, pat yourself on the back and keep it moving.

Level-up Challenge: Are you a perfectionist? You better ask somebody. This is not a reality show. It's time to uncover the real deal and release those toxic chains.

* * * * * * *

It's all about continuing to understand who you are, revealing the power that resides in you. This next section builds on those moments and pushes you to go deeper, so grab a journal, notepad, tablet, or laptop. By the way, these are all also Level-up Challenges for this chapter with brief reflection moments included.

Let's jump into the deep end of the pool. A life raft is waiting.

Let's discover when you're at your best!
Knowing when you are at your best helps you to be selective about the spaces you are in and inevitably, you will wind up in uncomfortable spaces. Knowing how to navigate this with some self-assessment will help manage expectations and also allow time to prepare and anticipate what's to come.

Finding Your Best Self

- Identify your unique strengths by journaling about a past experience where you felt confident, empowered, and in control.
- The experience could be an achievement, adversity, proud moment, or success in a business or personal setting.
- Make sure to use imagery and descriptive words that tell what happened and how you felt.
- If necessary, consult with others on those specific occasions to pull from them when they saw you shine. Once you are done, circle or highlight all of your positive qualities and strengths and use this knowledge to understand what type of environment you thrive in.

Finding Your Weaknesses

- Identify a past experience where you felt defeated, undervalued, or not in control of your emotions.
- The experience could be related to the workplace, business, or personal setting.
- Make sure to use imagery and descriptive words that tell you what happened and how you felt.
- If necessary, consult with others on that specific occasion and ask what they observed.

Once you are done, circle or highlight all of the areas and use this knowledge to understand challenging environments and your response. Find ways to mitigate stress in those situations. In the future, discern **where** you spend your time. Ask yourself if you needed to be there in the first place, i.e., use your power to delegate to someone else to attend the meeting/event and report back. Activate saying "NO" where you can and protect your peace at all costs.

Reflection: Winning can be defined as the science of being totally prepared, George Allen, Sr.

Flipping the Script on Negative Statements

During our lifetime, we are going to experience negativity, bad experiences, failures, and hurtful comments from people; you may have even repeatedly overlooked for promotions, but you cannot dwell on these incidents because this is another way to diminish your power if you do not build up a strong mental forcefield to deflect these offenses. Let's not confuse this with constructive criticism which, at times, can feel harsh as well. It is important to recognize how you will choose to handle these incidents because, in life, we are going to experience trials and tribulations. The more prepared you can be, the better off you'll be.

This will be a 4-week assignment. For each week, use a journal or notepad. Create three columns. Label the left column, "Offense" and note any judgments, accusations, hurtful statements, criticisms – anything that caused you angst, made you uneasy, or unhappy. Label the middle column, "Your Response/Feelings" and note your response and/or feelings to the Offense. And label the right column, "Learnings/Reflections" and note any learnings and/or reflections that came up for you. (*See sample below.*)

Offense	Your Response/ Feelings	Learnings/ Reflections
Your presentation was not well received	Defeated; embarrassed	Ask a trusted friend/ colleague to review future presentations
Being overlooked for promotion	Discounted; undervalued	Discuss with supervisor or re-evaluate if the job is the right fit or seek a new job

At the end of the 4 weeks, you should start to see a pattern that should help with your self-development but also, it should give you a clearer picture of how you deal with adversity.

Reflection - Learn to see the difference between constructive and destructive criticism. Appreciate the constructive, ignore the destructive. John Douglas.

Identify Your Core Beliefs

What is at the heart of who you are and what you believe? *Core beliefs can be defined as the very essence of how people see themselves, others, the world, and the future.*[2]

Take some time to note what you believe not just about yourself but about the environment around you. Really reflect on who you are in all of the capacities that you serve in – as a mother, wife, boss, leader, caregiver, etc. Core beliefs do not mean religious beliefs, although they could definitely serve as part of your belief system. What we're really drilling down into is where do you draw the line on a particular issue or topic? What are your morals? What makes you tick?

I want to challenge you to develop a Core Belief Statement for your own enlightenment. This will help to further identify your unique persona and validate the person in the mirror **for yourself**. Forming this statement will draw on your culture, upbringing, experiences, and other aspects of your life history. The best part about this is it will probably change as you continue to unpack and grow in your self-awareness, so don't think what you develop today is final. In fact, you should revisit your statement to make sure it still reflects who you are as you evolve.

In case this sounds daunting to you, I'm sharing my Core Belief statement below. I hope this helps you craft yours.

"I am a champion of women and students from all walks of life. Without my connection to my faith, I am nothing. I greatly value and love my family and my amazing circle of peers and friends. I am an advocate for the underdog and a giver of time, talent, and treasure. I believe everyone has value. All people of color should be fairly represented and deserve a seat at the table. I am a recovering perfectionist and will always seek excellence."

Reflection - Your attitude is an expression of your values, beliefs, and expectations. Brain Tracy

As a recap, this was about harnessing your power, but sister-friend, it is much more than that. I want you to embrace these key takeaways:

1. You have power! Power to mold, change, adapt, accept, influence, and make decisions.
2. Power is not only in the workplace; it's in your home, place of spiritual worship, school, neighborhood, and community.
3. Power resides in you, but you have to nurture it with life-giving energy through meditation, self-care, education, evaluation, just to name a few.
4. Power is visible! Walk with confidence. Show up as if you *deserve* a place at the table.
5. Power is a muscle. You have to exercise it and believe you can be ***the authority*** in applicable situations.
6. You have the Power to say NO!
7. Continually unpacking and working on your self-development can only reinforce and boost your self-assuredness, which ultimately will enhance your power.

Key 7: Tapping into the Source of Your Higher Power

There is a greater source/power that energizes and directs us on our journey. The one who finds it can achieve power.

Everything you have learned, all the actions you have done, will only get you to a certain level unless you have a connection to something greater than you. You can be leading the race and have a tire blow-out along the way. Who or what is at your pit stop? Primarily, we've focused on how to draw on your inner strength; we've talked about that circle of support -- having peers, family, and friends to lift you up and be there as your cheerleaders.

But there is something more than "people power." People are human with all their inherent frailties. With even the best intentions, the people factor will fail, misdirect, and falter. These days, people are operating on autopilot just trying to survive to the next day, so constantly depending on people will disappoint along the way, and that is nobody's fault.

No matter where you are on your journey of self-discovery, know that in this great circle of life there are other forces at work. For me, my prayer time is on point. Without my faith connection to God and Jesus Christ, I would not be the person I am today. My connection to a heavenly power has saved me countless times and has brought focus and clarity into my life that could not be achieved by reading books, attending seminars, or interacting with friends.

For some, it's Zen. Zen is both something we are, our true nature expressing itself moment by moment and something we do, a disciplined practice through which we can realize the joy of being. Zen…focuses on awareness through the practice of meditation. **Zen is slang for feeling peaceful and relaxed.**

Chi is another method that gives a connection to something other than yourself. Some believe that **Chi is a spiritual energy** that helps us to become physically stronger, mentally focused, energized, and revitalized.

As I stated, for me it is a faith-based spirituality, but it does not have to be for you; however, I strongly encourage you to understand you are not operating on your own volition. It's so important for you to be grounded in something *other than what you can see.*

Take the wind for example. It is invisible, yet it makes its presence known through cool breezes on a hot day or it can intensify cold on a blustery day. You know it's there with the swaying of the leaves or as it speaks using a howling whistle through the trees, yet it does not have a face. But it has a *spiritual force.*

What does it mean to be spiritual? The term tends to be closely associated with organized religion, but that is not the only viewpoint. This excerpt from an article from the

University of Minnesota provides an excellent definition that I hope speaks to you as well:

> *Spirituality is a broad concept with room for many perspectives. In general, it includes a sense of connection to something bigger than ourselves, and it typically involves **a search for meaning in life.***
>
> *Some may find that their spiritual life is intricately linked to their association with a church, temple, mosque, or synagogue. Others may pray or find comfort in a personal relationship with God or a higher power. **Still others seek meaning through their connections to nature or art.***

What we're talking about is WHAT or WHO gives you life. Why this is important is there will be many times when your friends, peers, and colleagues fail you and you feel hopeless with nowhere else to turn. Your business may collapse, your home foreclosed, your finances depleted, your marriage dissolved, and you will be left to deal with a lot of this on your own.

Without a connection to that higher power, you will surely feel empty because our mental and physical capacity to deal with adversity, disappointment, sadness, heartache, and stress does have a threshold. Not only does that external, universal connection refuel you during these times, but it works in reverse as well.

What that means is your successes should indeed be celebrated. But even when you're *living your life like it's golden* and everything is going according to plan, I firmly believe behind the scenes, there are a lot of forces in motion *that caused it to happen that way*, whether it was your political connections, savvy negotiating skills, business acumen, financial windfall – it didn't just happen without *something* putting the balls in motion to bounce in your favor.

Recognizing you are not an independent power source allows you to be humble. It allows you to not be selfish in your thinking or your ways. It compels you to embrace the connections around you and also work in communion with others. It is an attitude of gratitude for what you've been blessed with and further see how your contribution to the better good reverberates across all aisles.

If you've never thought about life in this way, I hope you're open to seeing how this way of thinking will help you be a better person for yourself and those around you. In essence, continually striving to find your "complete" power.

Remember the definition of spirituality from the beginning:

- a search for meaning in life
- spiritual life linked to association with a church, temple, mosque, or synagogue
- connections to nature or art

These descriptions should really speak to your soul, and they are broad enough to give you plenty of leeway with your spiritual walk.

If you are still unsure how to make that higher connection, there are multiple options below. Reflect on which ones are best for you and test drive a few.

1. **Meditation.** Just take some quiet time to sit still and just listen. Doing this will not only help to sustain you in your natural, mental and emotional strength, but it will give you that super boost to help fulfill your purpose.

2. **Surrounding Yourself in Nature.** A trip to the mountains, botanical gardens, farms, aquariums, conservatories, etc. will help you appreciate just how vast and varied our world is and how you are just one small part of it.

3. **Retreats.** Taking a solo retreat that is designed to connect to your inner self and also retreats that intentionally reduce or eliminate external communication (social media, television, phone) forces you to really be in tune and self-reflect.

4. **Yoga.** Yoga is a type of exercise in which you move your body into various positions to become more fit or flexible, improve breathing, and relax your mind. The fundamental purpose is to foster harmony in the body, mind, and environment. Yoga professes a complete system of physical, mental, social, and spiritual development.

5. **Hiking/Walking/Jogging.** Walking and taking hikes is not only great exercise, but it allows you to get moving! It gives you time to just enjoy nature, your neighborhood, meet/greet new people and relax your mind so you can handle whatever is next on life's agenda.

6. **Consistent Prayer Life.** Finding solace and comfort in the word of God is a great place to find all answers to life's circumstances.

7. **Solitude.** Just find time to just BE. Pack a bag and go to a nearby hotel or retreat center and clear your

mind from all stress and sorrow. Focus on who you are in that moment and just allow your thoughts to roam at will. See what clarity and energy you gain just by being alone.

8. **Music and the Arts.** Sometimes the right song, movie, play, or book hits you just right; a lot of people find jazz soothing. For this one, I encourage you to connect to those mediums that are inspirational, encouraging, faith-based, or educational. Dancing is another great release.

9. **Solo Travel.** Similar to #7, schedule quick day trips, weekend getaways, or extended vacations alone. Go someplace new. Have an agenda or wing it; the point is not to be tied down unless you want to be and let life show you which way to go vs. you are always trying to run things. Be FREE.

10. **Rest and Relaxation.** There is something to be said for a good night's sleep and/or not feeling like you have to get up, get dressed, and "do" something. Turn off that alarm clock, order in, lock the door, and really allow your body to naturally heal and rejuvenate.

Each one of these will provide you an opportunity to find what is your kinetic energy source that will sustain and refill your tank. This energy source needs to be integrated into your life so you have something to lean on when life throws you curveballs with no end in sight. This connection will be in your toolkit to help you realign, readjust, and bring you back to your center zone.

For example, if you've had a rough day, you may say, "I need to go for a walk to clear my head." Or you may say, "Salsa dancing really helps me feel alive and energized." I know people who jog regularly and are no good without that routine exercise. It's their connection to something **outside of themselves** that invigorates them and allows them to move on.

If none of these speak your language, I encourage you to talk with others, but not just anyone. Seek out those who you know are going through hardships and pain, yet when you see them, they are smiling, laughing, being engaging, looking pristine, and handling their business. Trust and believe there is something that is allowing them to persevere – something that is carrying them when they are weak, pushing them out of bed, giving them a sound mind and body. Ask them **who** is at their pit stop when the wheels fall off. Their answers may surprise you but also enlighten and inspire you to know there are greater forces at work and through our humanity, all things are connected.

Motivational Moment

Look back over your life and note those moments where you were like, "Wow, I don't know how I survived." Then meditate and look at the events leading up to and afterward. Ask yourself what did you learn, who or what do you see in the midst of your challenge? If you journal, then journal your thoughts on these questions and answers.

Level-up Challenge

Regardless of your religious or spiritual beliefs, I challenge you to attend a service or event of a different religion than yourself or if you are not associated with any one religion, go with a trusted friend to one of their services or events and just observe any similarities or differences. If this is too much of a stretch, seek out spiritual readings and/or talks by experts on the subject of spirituality and note any key takeaways that apply to your life.

The Final Keynote

The journey is great; don't forget to enjoy it on the way to your goal.

We never finish unpacking on our journey to becoming the best version of ourselves. You're constantly evolving and growing, discovering your uniqueness and refining your place in the world. If you believe you have already unlocked your full potential, I want to challenge you to look deeper. We are like a sweet onion that has multiple layers. As you peel back your own layers, each one will reveal something new and enlightening to help you come into alignment with your purpose. Everything we are meant to be is already inside of us; it just has to be unpacked.

I offer four final messages below, each one focused on different stages of life, for each stage offers new beginnings, hope, opportunities, and reflection. I encourage you to read each one as they are building blocks regardless of where you are on your current journey.

To the Amazing Young College Student (18 – 24)

You are just at the beginning of your adult life. It may seem as if you know everything there is to know; after all, you're an adult, but there is so much more ahead of you. There will be so many roads you'll travel and during these early stages of your life, you'll be constantly unpacking different choices. Sometimes the options will be confusing. Up until this point, as a high-school student, you may have had the guidance and protection of your parents or siblings, along with their best advice. Your teachers and guidance office did a lot of handholding and follow-up in an effort to help you succeed. But in college, most *or all* of that goes away. If you don't show up for class, no one is going to call you. If you fail exams, there are no parent-teacher conferences. There will be a lot of "noise" in your head from other students, trying to sway you in one direction or another, dangling all sorts of keys in your direction. It's so easy to get mixed up because sometimes we can make our keys open the wrong doors. In other words, we force the key to jam it open instead of waiting for it to click.

Freedom comes at a price with lots of discernment: You are unpacking the right friendships, deciding on a field of study, dating, relationships, and just beginning to understand how you handle stress, independence, and adversity. After four years, there will be new decisions: Should you go to graduate school? Start a career? Get married? These life decisions may seem far away, but four years will be in your rearview mirror before you know it.

I want you to be prepared for what lies ahead. All of the keys provided in this book are to help you advance in your personal and professional life. If you work continually on your self-improvement, it will help you to better navigate life's journey. These seven keys have power, but only if you apply them to your life.

My hope for you is that you will not let anyone, or anything, hinder your growth during this very pivotal time of your life and that you will take advantage of every opportunity to excel and exceed your goals. Pursue that which will make you happy. Chasing dollars without joy in what you're doing can bring a lot of stress, so choose wisely. Do not be afraid to shed friends you may have outgrown, especially if they are causing a distraction. True friends will encourage and cheerlead you on to power no matter what.

Chapter(s) For Review:

· Key 2 – Discovering Your Why
· Key 3 - The Journey to Self-Discovery
· Key 6 - Harnessing Your Power
· Key 7 - Tapping into the Source of Your Higher Power

To the Phenomenal Professional Woman (25 – 40)

· *This range is extensive, as it covers two time periods: the younger postgraduate woman and the established professional. We will start with the postgraduate woman.*

The Postgraduate Career Woman (25 – 30)

You are out of college and have started to be a young professional. You've gone from one world -- the academic world, to the next world: the unforgiving workforce. College was somewhat of a safe environment. Now the stakes are higher. Decisions are longer lasting and more impactful. You're trying to find where you fit in this new transition from pulling all-nighters, partying, and eating ramen noodles to where a whole new set of rules exist. You are the newbie on the block and some of your colleagues will be welcoming while others will be expecting you to earn your dues. It will be competitive, as you learn the unwritten rules and policies in your new position. There are a lot of players in this board game, and you haven't been given the rules . Some will steer you in the right direction and others won't, so **learn the game for yourself**. Do a lot of research. Take time to listen and observe. Know when to ask questions and what questions to ask.

During this time, it will be important for you to **exude confidence**. Now is not the time to fall to the back of the line. If you don't have the confidence, they will eat you alive. I want you to remember **that you belong there**. It's okay to be nervous but do not allow your anxiety to outshine your power. You will encounter different keys that will open doors, some with a safety net and some without.

From college until now, you are unpacking different sets of keys. You're finding out: I'm the type of person that is detailed oriented, I'm able to do dynamic presentations, I'm great at managing, I'm able to interpret complex proposals, and so on. There are so many other skillsets you will develop to further your career and be promoted. It is inevitable, but you will encounter haters, yet you will have knowledge on how to deal with them. You've got to get ahead of those who seek to dim your light and not be afraid to let your light beam bright. You do this by being present and secure in your place at the table. You are not only professional in the way you express yourself and with the quality work you produce, but also in the way you look and carry yourself. Invest in office-appropriate work attire so you are always ready for that high-powered meeting or dream interview. Dress for the career you want, not the one you have.

If you let your guard down, they will take advantage of it because they will see your laid-back demeanor and lack of tenacity as incompetent and worse yet, that you don't belong here. Passive aggressiveness may work in relationships (to keep the peace, but never recommended because you should be able to bring your true self to a relationship), but in the workplace where you are trying to make your mark, that characteristic will not serve you well. Next thing you know, you are quitting and going somewhere else and that will be a habitual pattern because haters are here to stay! You have to let them be the energy to your progress and promotion.

I want to share an important eye-opener related to this. Sometimes we flee an uncomfortable situation because we do not like confrontation, or we may have to deal with people who are not nice or situations that seem awkward or uncomfortable. You should not be job-hopping until you have discerned that where you are is not your divine path because the more you live into your destiny, the more obstacles will come your way. This is why it is important to reflect, meditate, and assess your self-development. Do the work and stay prepared.

My hope for you as you crossover into this new dimension of being a professional is that you make strategic steps to your power. Do not get intimidated by your new surroundings. Notice what works and what doesn't work; align yourself with like-minded individuals and those who can help you grow. Use the seven keys as they all work together **for your good.**

The Established Professional (30 – 40)

Now that you've been in the corporate, business, entrepreneurial or academic setting for a few years, you are no longer considered the "new kid on the block," although there are always twists and turns as we navigate life. At this stage, however, the rules of the game should be coming into alignment. You know when to speak your mind in a more eloquent way because you now see how you fit into the big picture. There should be less stress and anxiety from haters and naysayers and more confidence and power about how to deal with those personality types so that you do not feel like the victim but the victor! It's important that as you mature, you also grow and transform mentally into a protected place of peace.

Also, during this time, you will probably have developed a new circle of work "friends." Though you can make some lifelong friends from coworkers, it becomes more about **trust.** Sure, there will be business outings to attend together, but be very much aware of your environment. Especially early on, it's not recommended to mix the two -- work and business. You need to guard yourself and be savvy about how much you share and **with whom**. Everybody doesn't have to know everything about you. Use discretion and discernment with what you share with people.

There's a popular saying: Some people are in your life for a reason, a season, or a lifetime. Don't despair if a few people fall off your "friend" list because if they dropped off that easily, were they really a friend to begin with? Friends can also be frenemies (a mashup of friend-enemies). They could be hanging around just to see your every move and then sabotaging you behind the scenes.

As you allow people to have access to you, really ask yourself: How do they fit into your life? Are they an asset or a liability? This could really be a game-changer, like is your circle one of promotion (uplifting and empowering) or demotion (toxic and pessimistic)? If it's the latter, an evaluation is in order.

Another area where you should be focusing on is seeking professional development. Start assessing how you are going to bolster your CV. During performance management sessions, look to build on training, classes, and certifications. Collaborate with your supervisor on a career path that will not only set you up for success but will consistently build your toolbox with desirable transferable skill sets.

Whether you are physically in the office, teleworking, or working in the home, you still need to create a harmonious environment where there is balance. **Balance does not mean 50/50.** It's a distribution that is holistically in tune with who you are and what your needs are. Make sure you are creating a quality lifestyle, where you are not doing everything for everybody under the sun and are burnt out by sundown. Recalibrate tasks and do not be afraid to delegate so that you have time to breathe and nurture your other talents. Your day job may not be your passion, so make sure you make room for those other gifts which may become your main source of joy and livelihood.

Chapter(s) For Review:

- Key 3: The Journey to Self-Discovery
- Key 4: The Key to Overcoming Haters
- Key 7: Tapping into the Source of Your Higher Power

For the Outstanding Seasoned Professional Woman (40+).
At this different chapter of your life, you're now at the point where you have sustained enough professional and personal battle wounds. You have probably gone through some things that have redefined who you are as a person. You know all about the haters and have played that game, but playtime is over. You're more comfortable in your own skin and have no qualms about speaking your truth, tactfully, of course. You are also uncovering some other new layers about yourself that didn't surface at the younger or new professional stage. At this era of your life, there may be some reflecting on making some new decisions on what direction you want to pursue with a comfortable retirement in mind.

Life has its twists and turns, each having different and lasting effects. Losing family or friends, job changes, health issues, having a family, being a caregiver, etc., are major life events that can bring turmoil and strife but there is also happiness. This is also the making of who you are constantly becoming.

You've unpacked some keys and unlocked some doors but...there are some doors that may have remained locked. No matter how hard you've tried, no matter how many keys you've put in, you have not been able to see that door opening. Because of those doors being shut, frustration may have set in dreams deferred or denied. Frustration can be a demon that needs to be tamed.

For you, the deeper, internal in-depth reflection becomes vital because there are probably more years behind you than ahead of you. Be intentional about meditating and reflecting, so you can re-evaluate decisions you've made. Finding your peace, tranquility, and ways to meditate and connect spiritually is vitally important. At this point, you start to reevaluate your life and things you did, how it looked, and decisions you made that maybe you shouldn't have. This can be eye-opening, but do not let it deter you from moving forward.

This range of emotions is normal. Looking back and seeing where you've been should be done more often than not. It's a good way to celebrate how far you've come and open the door to planning for where you still hope to go. These moments help to reconfirm and uncover new keys and new layers. At this age, you may feel like there is no reason to keep pressing forward with a new vision or new plans, but there is always room for more until **you** close the door. You are still alive and anything that doesn't continue to be fed will wither away and perish. Feed your mind with knowledge; feed your body with good nutrients and feed your soul with self-care.

My hope is that you never get complacent. Because you've been out there for so long, you may feel like there's nothing new to do, but always look to move ahead. Do not be hindered by circumstances, family, or friends. There's still a lot more to learn. Forty is the new thirty and fifty is the new forty. Do not allow your age at this stage to define your next move. Do it, even though you may be afraid, and start today.

Chapter(s) for Review:

· **Key 1**: Dealing with Demons in Your Suitcase
· **Key 7**: Tapping into the Source of Your Higher Power

For the Retired Woman with Vitality

Whether you've retired in your golden years or were blessed to retire earlier, maybe now you're able to do what you always wanted to do. Your keys may start to look a little different, but the road to discovery does not stop. As long as you have breath, you can still open new doors.

This age group has changed dramatically over the years. Retirees can be a range of ages doing many amazing things, such as going back to school, teaching, mentoring, and some have even become entrepreneurs. This is not about what "box" you fit in. You can self-identify across many categories.

If you are indeed retired, make sure you plan to enjoy the fruit of your labor. You have given your time, talent, and energy. Do your best to keep moving both physically and mentally. At this stage, your self-discovery should be clearer and who you are should be well-defined.

My **hope** for you is that you can do what your heart desires, whether that means taking a nap in the middle of the day, traveling, visiting family, taking care of the grand-kids, or other activities. Impart keys of wisdom (mentor another sister on her journey) to those who will come behind you, as you are now the shoulders they will stand on with aspirations to be able to get to a place of retirement.

Chapter(s) for Review:

· Key 7: Tapping into the Source of Your Higher Power

In Conclusion

Depending on where you are in life, I want you to strive to be a lifelong learner. There will be trials and errors, successes and failures, some wins and a few losses, but through it all, you'll be continually unlocking your keys to power.

Take time to really discover who you are. If someone asks, "What makes you happy?" you should be able to respond without a second thought and if you can't, it's a tell-tale sign you're still on your journey of self-discovery and not doing the proper self-care, no doubt, taking care of everyone else. You are important. This has nothing to do with being self-centered. It's more about being your best self and doing the work to get there. You should always want to project the best YOU no matter the situation, but you can't bring your best self if you are constantly putting yourself last.

You must replenish your mind, body, and soul. You can't pour out of an empty cup. So always remember that YOU MATTER. You deserve to excel and thrive in life. Stop just surviving. It doesn't matter how it used to look, where you began, or where you came from. It matters where you are right now and where you plan to go from here. Start where you are and GROW!

You deserve to win.

About Dr. Kim

Dr. Kim is a faith-filled, successful businesswoman, councilwoman, Vice Mayor and longtime educational leader with a strong commitment to equity and inclusion. As an advocate for university students and women leadership, her passion and commitment over the last seventeen years have focused on several areas including: increasing diversity, closing the achievement gap, academic excellence, preparation, women advocacy in various aspects and motivation.

Currently, Dr. Kim serves as director of higher education, where she continues to enhance diversity and inclusion for underrepresented students and first generation students and afford them the opportunity to achieve success at every academic level. She is also part of several boards and organizations that impact and empower women nationally and internationally.

She received a bachelor's degree from Hampton University, a master's degree from the University of Maryland, and a Doctorate with a focus on Public Policy and Social Change from Union Institute and University.

Today, as the CEO and Founder of *Journey To Becoming* and author of *Unlock Your Power*, Dr. Kim aims to inspire students, women and girls who are inspiring to find their power, thought leaders and change agents on a global scale to live fulfilled, powerful lives.

Dr. Kim serves on several committees and meets regularly with influencers and decision-makers to impact change in the community.

During her downtime, Dr. Kim mentors women and college students and enjoys traveling and the arts, especially dance and music. Her mantra is never to give up and to be grateful for life. She lives by, "Life is short; enjoy and appreciate every part of it."

Additionally, she hosted a podcast called, "#Becomer Series" promoting women and others who support women in achieving their goals. Furthermore, she co-hosted a live-stream show with Rochel Lawson called "Real Talk" designed with the mindset of connecting, inspiring, motivating, supporting, and uniting women around the world. It is a safe place where women can come together to discuss the "Real" issues and challenges that women face in today's society. It has been designed to be a safe place where women can share their wisdom, receive wisdom, and talk about what we can do to make the world a better place.

Connect with Dr. Brown at power@allthingsdrkim.com